TELLING Your Friends ABOUT CHRIST

A 4-week cou
highers build
ability to tell friends about

by Christine Yount

Group
Loveland, Colorado

Telling Your Friends About Christ

Copyright © 1991 by Group Publishing, Inc.

First Printing

Credits
Edited by Stephen Parolini
Cover designed by Jill Christopher and DeWain Stoll
Interior designed by Judy Bienick and Jan Aufdemberge
Illustrations on pp. 3, 28, 35, 44 and 48 by Bruce Tilsley
Illustrations on pp. 5, 9 and 19 by Rick Stromoski

ISBN 1-55945-114-9
Printed in the United States of America

CONTENTS

Help kids understand their friends' need for Christ.

Help kids understand how to reach out in love to others.

Help kids know how to tell others about God's love.

Help kids each develop their own style of telling others about Christ.

TELLING YOUR FRIENDS ABOUT CHRIST

Evangelistic Broadcast Reaches Millions

Door-to-Door Visiting Brings in Hundreds

Thousands Follow Christ in Evangelistic Crusade

Boy Expelled from School for Preaching

When kids consider telling their friends about Christ, they often think of the approaches described in the above headlines. Kids feel either inadequate for, or scared to death of, the task. Kids also worry they may have to do something weird, such as standing on a street corner and preaching to strangers.

Although much of Jesus' ministry was to crowds of strangers, his closest friends were his closest followers. Jesus used relationships to help people make strong faith commitments to him. Jesus doesn't often ask his followers to do anything weird or outrageous. He asks his followers to love their friends and tell them about him.

But kids don't often see the value of mixing faith with friendship. Consider the statistics in the box on page 5. Kids want to make friends—but don't feel comfortable telling friends about their faith.

Kids deal with some hefty obstacles when it comes to telling their friends about Christ: "What if my friends reject me?" "What if I say the wrong thing?" "How do I even start talking about my beliefs?"

Junior highers are struggling to find and develop friendships. They may fear that telling friends about Christ would threaten their developing friendships. They need to be reassured that there are many non-threatening ways to tell someone about their faith.

According to Recent Surveys ...

- 75% of young people say they want to know more about how to make friends and be friends ...

... but 47% of those young people say they rarely or never talk to their best friends about faith or God.

- 82% of young people say they know God wants them to tell others about Christ ...

... but only 25% say they've tried to bring up the subject of their beliefs to anyone.

Kids also feel insecure with their communication skills. As they develop into young adults, kids often trip over words and stumble through conversations—afraid they might say the wrong thing. Kids need to learn the basics of their faith so they can confidently tell it to others.

With *Telling Your Friends About Christ*, kids will see how Jesus reached out to his friends. Students will learn how they can overcome obstacles to tell their friends about Jesus. This course will give kids the methods and perspective they need to effectively reach out to their friends.

Get involved with your kids in this 4-week course. Share your failures and successes in telling *your* friends about Christ. Walk along with your kids as they reach out to their friends. As you apply the things you learn in this course, you'll be the greatest "object lesson" of all.

During this course, your students will:
- understand that they can make a difference in the world;
- learn that everyone needs Christ's forgiveness;
- see how Christ reached out through relationships;
- be able to tell how being a Christian has made a difference in their lives;
- learn to tell others about Jesus' message; and
- identify specific friends they want to tell about Christ.

COURSE OBJECTIVES

HOW TO USE THIS COURSE

Think back on an important lesson you've learned in life. Did you learn it from reading about it? from hearing about it? from something you experienced? Chances are, the most important lessons you've learned came from something you experienced. That's what active learning is—learning by doing. And active learning is a key element in Group's Active Bible Curriculum.

Active learning leads students in doing things that help them understand important principles, messages and ideas. It's a discovery process that helps kids internalize what they learn.

Each lesson section in Group's Active Bible Curriculum plays an important part in active learning:

The **Opener** involves kids in the topic in fun and unusual ways.

The **Action and Reflection** includes an experience designed to evoke specific feelings in the students. This section also processes those feelings through "How did you feel?" questions, and applies the message to situations kids face.

The **Bible Application** actively connects the topic with the Bible. It helps kids see how the Bible's message is relevant to the situations they face.

The **Commitment** helps students internalize the Bible's message and commit to make changes in their lives.

The **Closing** funnels the lesson's message into a time of creative reflection and prayer.

When you put all the sections together, you get a lesson that's fun to teach. And kids get messages they'll remember.

BEFORE THE 4-WEEK SESSION

● Read the introduction, the Course Objectives and This Course at a Glance.

● Decide how you'll publicize the course using the clip art on the Publicity Page (p. 9). Prepare fliers, newsletter articles and posters as needed.

● Look at the Bonus Ideas (p. 45) and decide which ones you'll use.

- Read the opening statements, Objectives and Bible Basis for the lesson. The Bible Basis shows how specific passages relate to junior highers today.

- Choose which Opener and Closing options to use. Each is appropriate for a different kind of group. The first option is often more active.

- Gather necessary supplies from This Lesson at a Glance.

- Read each section of the lesson. Adjust where necessary for your class size and meeting room.

BEFORE EACH LESSON

- The approximate minutes listed give you an idea of how long each activity will take. Each lesson is designed to take 35 to 60 minutes. Shorten or lengthen activities as needed to fit your group.

- If you see you're going to have extra time, do an activity or two from the "If You Still Have Time . . ." box or from the Bonus Ideas (p. 45).

- Since this is a course on telling others about Christ, it's assumed that the participants are all Christians. But that may not be the case in your class. If you've got one or more non-Christians in your class, be aware that they may feel uncomfortable with some of the activities.

Encourage non-Christian kids to participate in all activities, but don't force them to do something that goes against their beliefs. Who knows, as Christian kids talk about their faith, the non-Christian kids may respond by asking how to become Christians!

- Dive into the activities with the kids. Don't be a spectator. The lesson will be more successful and rewarding to you and your students.

HELPFUL HINTS

- The answers given after discussion questions are responses your students *might* give. They aren't the only answers or the "right" answers. If needed, use them to spark discussion. Kids won't always say what you wish they'd say. That's why some of the responses given are negative or controversial. If someone responds negatively, don't be shocked. Accept the person, and use the opportunity to explore other angles of the issue.

THIS COURSE AT A GLANCE

Before you dive into the lessons, familiarize yourself with each lesson aim. Then read the scripture passages.
- Study them as a background to the lessons.
- Use them as a basis for your personal devotions.
- Think about how they relate to kids' circumstances today.

LESSON 1: A FRIEND IN NEED

Lesson Aim: To help kids understand their friends' need for Christ.

Bible Basis: Luke 5:1-11, 27-28; John 1:35-51; and Romans 3:23; 5:6-8.

LESSON 2: CAUGHT IN A WEB OF LOVE

Lesson Aim: To help kids understand how to reach out in love to others.

Bible Basis: Matthew 20:26-28; Romans 10:13-15; and Philippians 2:3-4.

LESSON 3: BRIDGE-BUILDING

Lesson Aim: To help kids know how to tell others about God's love.

Bible Basis: John 3:16 and 1 Corinthians 15:3-4.

LESSON 4: LOOK WHO'S TALKING

Lesson Aim: To help kids each develop their own style of telling others about Christ.

Bible Basis: Matthew 16:18 and John 3:1—4:54.

PUBLICITY PAGE

Grab your junior highers' attention! Photocopy this page, then cut out and paste the clip art of your choice in your church bulletin or newsletter to advertise this course on telling friends about Christ. Or photocopy and use the ready-made flier as a bulletin insert. Permission to photocopy this clip art is granted for local church use.

Splash the clip art on posters, fliers or even postcards! Just add the vital details: the date and time the course begins and where you'll meet.

It's that simple.

TELLING Your Friends **ABOUT CHRIST**

TELLING Your Friends **ABOUT CHRIST**

TELLING YOUR **FRIENDS** ABOUT **CHRIST**

Come learn how to effectively tell others about your faith in God!

Come to

On

At

A FRIEND IN NEED

Who needs Jesus? People in faraway lands, drug addicts, AIDS victims—yes. But sometimes kids are blind to their own friends' need for Christ. Kids need to understand it's not how "good" a person seems that determines his or her need for Christ; it's how "human" a person is. Everyone needs God's gift of eternal life.

To help kids understand their friends' need for Christ.

LESSON AIM

Students will:
- **understand that everyone needs Christ's forgiveness;**
- **realize the importance of being someone's friend;**
- **learn how Christ reached out through relationships; and**
- **pray to be effective in telling others about Christ.**

OBJECTIVES

Look up the following scriptures. Then read the background paragraphs to see how the passages relate to your junior highers and middle schoolers.

In **Luke 5:1-11, 27-28** and **John 1:35-51**, Jesus uses natural relationship ties to reach out to his disciples.

When kids think of Jesus' ministry, they often picture him preaching to crowds, feeding the multitudes, healing the sick or casting out demons. To them, Jesus probably seems more like a crusade evangelist than a friend.

These verses, however, show how Jesus built relationships with his disciples. And through those relationships, he built more relationships. The intimate relationships proved to be the strongest. Jesus called Peter and his brother Andrew to follow him; they brought along James and John; Andrew also brought his friend Philip, who brought his friend Nathanael; then Matthew the "IRS man" followed also.

BIBLE BASIS
LUKE 5:1-11, 27-28
JOHN 1:35-51
ROMANS 3:23, 5:6-8

Kids need to see their friends, family members and acquaintances as potential followers of Christ. When they see that telling others about Christ involves already-established relationships, they'll be less intimidated.

In **Romans 3:23** and **5:6-8**, Paul says everyone has sinned and that Jesus died for sinners.

The consequence of sin is death. But Jesus died in the place of sinners. It wasn't because we're so lovable that Christ died for us—it was because he's so loving.

By understanding there's no such thing as "us and them" when it comes to sin, kids can develop a more humble attitude toward their non-Christian friends. They can also see their friends' need for Christ more clearly, and therefore be more willing to overcome obstacles to tell friends about Christ.

THIS LESSON AT A GLANCE

Section	Minutes	What Students Will Do	Supplies
Opener (Option 1)	5 to 10	**The Need of the World**—Take a look at sin in the world.	Newspapers, tape, Bible
(Option 2)		**The Weight of Sin**—Decide if they want everyone to know their sins.	Bathroom scales, Bible
Action and Reflection	10 to 15	**Rainbow Bubbles**—Experience how it feels to be left out.	Bubble gum, newsprint, markers
Bible Application	10 to 15	**Jesus' Relationships**—See how Jesus reached out through relationships.	"Relationships—Jesus Style" handouts (p. 18), pencils, Bibles, tape, newsprint, markers
Commitment	5 to 10	**You Never . . .**—Write letters to hurting friends.	Paper, pencils
Closing (Option 1)	5 to 10	**Relationship Sculptures**—Create sculptures to remind them to tell friends about Christ.	Posterboard, scissors, tape, markers
(Option 2)		**Talk and Pray**—Tell each other what qualities make them effective in telling others about Christ.	

The Lesson

☐ OPTION 1: THE NEED OF THE WORLD

Form groups of no more than four. Distribute newspapers to each group. Have kids read through the newspapers and tear out articles that show the effects of sin in the world: crime, sexual misconduct, cheating, war, scandals. Have kids in each group tape their articles on their clothing. Encourage kids to collect as many stories as possible.

Then have groups each briefly describe situations in articles they found.

Read aloud Romans 3:23 and 5:6-8.

Ask:

● **What do these verses say about sin?** (Everyone has sinned; everyone needs Jesus.)

● **How does it make you feel to be called a sinner?** (Dirty; angry; okay.)

● **How do the newspaper articles we taped on ourselves change our appearance?** (We look stupid; we look trashy.)

● **How is that like what sin does to us?** (Sin makes us feel bad; sin gets in the way of our relationship with God; sin is ugly.)

Say: **The Bible says everyone has sinned and needs forgiveness. Today we're going to talk about how your own friends need Jesus.**

☐ OPTION 2: THE WEIGHT OF SIN

Set a bathroom scale on the floor.

Say: **This scale reveals all the pounds you've gained in your lifetime. Nothing is hidden. How comfortable would you feel stepping onto this scale and letting everyone see your weight?**

Have volunteers tell how they'd feel. Be sensitive to kids who are overweight or underweight, and don't force people to tell how they'd feel. If kids are reluctant to tell how they'd feel, ask them to think of friends who'd be comfortable or uncomfortable standing on the scale.

Ask:

● **Why are some people uncomfortable with telling others their weight, age, grades or other "private" things?** (They're embarrassed; it's no one else's business.)

Have one or two volunteers stand on the scale, and loudly announce their weight.

Place another bathroom scale beside the first one, and say: **This scale reveals all the sins you've committed in your lifetime. Nothing is hidden. Now, those of you who are willing to have everyone know all your sins, stand on my** right. If you're unwilling, stand on my left.

Most kids will probably stand on your left. Ask:

● **Why did you stand on the side you did?** (I didn't want anyone to know my sins; I haven't done anything that bad.)

● **How did you feel when you thought your sins might be revealed?** (Embarrassed; scared; like I wanted to laugh.)

Read aloud Romans 3:23 and 5:6-8.

Ask:

● **What do these verses say about sin?** (Everyone has sinned; everyone needs Jesus.)

Say: **We all feel the weight of sin from time to time. But the good news we read in Romans tells us Jesus died to take away our sins. We can share that good news with our friends.**

Table Talk

The Table Talk activity in this course helps junior highers and middle schoolers discuss with their parents how to tell others about Christ.

If you choose to use the Table Talk activity, this is a good time to show students the "Table Talk" handout (p. 19). Ask them to spend time with their parents completing it.

Before kids leave, give them each them each the "Table Talk" handout to take home, or tell them you'll send it to their parents.

Or use the Table Talk idea found in the Bonus Ideas (p. 46) for a meeting based on the handout.

ACTION AND REFLECTION

(10 to 15 minutes)

RAINBOW BUBBLES

Distribute different-color bubble gum to kids. For example, you might give out five pieces of green bubble gum, five pieces of pink, one piece of blue and one piece of white. Arrange it so you have groups of at least three kids with same-color bubble gum, and at least two kids with unique colors that don't match any others. Tell kids not to let anyone see the color of their bubble gum.

On "go," have kids each chew their gum, blow a bubble and find others with the same color bubble. When kids find others with the same color, have them all blow a bubble at the same time and sit down.

After groups have formed, two (or more) people will be alone.

Ask the kids without a group:

● **How did you feel when you didn't fit in anywhere?** (Left out; mad, I thought it was unfair; I didn't care.)

Ask everyone:

● **How did you feel when you saw the people left out of your groups?** (Embarrassed; I felt sorry for them; sad.)

● **How is that like how you feel about friends who aren't Christian?** (Sometimes I feel sorry for non-Christians; I'm embarrassed about non-Christian friends; I'm sad when I think about friends who don't know Jesus.)

● **What are ways we exclude non-Christians?** (We don't talk about Christ with them; we don't invite them to church events.)

Form groups of no more than five. Give groups each a sheet of newsprint and a marker. Have kids brainstorm ways to bring up the topic of faith with their friends. For example, kids might suggest inviting a friend to a church event or asking a friend what he or she thinks about God. Have groups each list their ideas on the newsprint. Then have them each present their list to the rest of the class.

Ask:

● **Is it easier to tell a friend or a stranger about Christ? Explain.** (A friend, because friends trust what you believe; a stranger, because you can be bold with someone you don't know and may not see again.)

Say: **Jesus included his friends in the most important aspect of his life—his faith. And we can do the same thing. We can include our friends in faith discussions, and introduce them to the Christian faith. Let's see how Jesus used relationships to share his message with others.**

JESUS' RELATIONSHIPS

Form groups of no more than four. Give kids each a "Relationships—Jesus Style" handout (p. 18), a pencil and a Bible. Have kids each complete the handout. Then have groups each discuss the completed handouts.

While kids are completing their handouts, tape a sheet of newsprint to the wall for each group. After groups are finished, give kids each a different-color marker. Have a volunteer from each group draw a stick figure to represent Jesus in the center of his or her group's newsprint. One at a time, have kids go to their newsprint and draw the relationship web they drew earlier on their handout. Have kids look for relationships they share with other kids and draw connecting lines from themselves to those people.

After the webs are completed, read aloud Matthew 28:18-20.

Ask:

● **How is telling our friends about Christ a way of fulfilling the mission in this passage?** (Friends are part of the "nations" we're supposed to teach; telling friends about Christ is a way of teaching them.)

Say: **Today we've learned how Jesus used his relationships with others to tell them his message. No matter who we tell about Christ, when we openly talk about our faith we're fulfilling Jesus' command to make disciples of all nations.**

BIBLE APPLICATION
(10 to 15 minutes)

COMMITMENT
(5 to 10 minutes)

YOU NEVER . . .

Kids may not fully realize the important impact they can have on non-Christian friends. They may think "someone else will tell them about Christ" instead of taking responsibility for telling friends about their faith. The "Letter From a Hurting Friend" is designed to help kids think about how important their role is in telling friends about Christ.

Read aloud the "Letter From a Hurting Friend." Ask kids each to imagine the letter was written to them. Afterward, give kids each a sheet of paper and a pencil. Form pairs and have partners talk about how the letter makes them feel. Then have partners each write a letter to a non-Christian friend, telling the friend about God's love. Have partners show their letters to each other and talk about them. Have kids each say one thing they like about their partner's letter; for example: "I like the way you wrote your letter" or "I like the way you're honest in your letter."

Letter From a Hurting Friend

Dear Christian Friend:

Remember me? I'm the friend you used to listen to music with for hours; pig out on pizza with until we were sick; and hang out with until my mom would threaten to make it official and just adopt you.

You used to tell me all your secrets . . . well, most of them.

When I was sad, you never told me Jesus could give me joy.

When I was scared, you never told me Jesus could give me courage.

When I was lonely, you never mentioned Jesus wanted to be with me always.

When I was deciding whether to use drugs, you never told me Jesus could give me wisdom.

And when I was alive, you never told me Jesus could give me eternal life.

You Never Told Me,
A Hurting Friend

CLOSING
(5 to 10 minutes)

☐ OPTION 1: RELATIONSHIP SCULPTURES

Give kids each some tape, a pair of scissors and sheet of posterboard.

Say: **Use your supplies to create a sculpture that represents your friendships. You might create a basketball team to represent playing basketball with your friends, or a smiling face to represent having fun with your friends.**

Give kids four minutes to create their sculptures. Be sure to do one yourself. Then have kids each explain their sculpture for the rest of the class.

Form a circle and say: **Each person has different reasons for enjoying his or her friends. But whatever the reasons, it's important to be honest with friends about our Christian faith and about God's love.**

Silently, use a black marker to draw a simple cross on your

sculpture. Pass the marker around the circle and have kids each draw a cross on their sculpture too.

Close in prayer, saying: **Dear God, thank you for friends. Help us to remember always to shine with your love when we're with our friends. Just as we've each placed a cross on our sculpture, let us each remember to tell our friends about Jesus' sacrifice on the cross. Amen.**

Have kids each go around and shake hands with at least three other kids, saying "You can make a difference in your friends' lives." Encourage kids to keep their sculptures as reminders to tell friends about Christ.

☐ OPTION 2: TALK AND PRAY

Form pairs. Have partners each describe a quality that'll make their partner effective in telling friends about Christ. For example, someone might say: "Your patience will help you talk with non-Christian friends" or "Your caring attitude will help you tell someone about Christ." Then have partners pray together that they'll be effective in telling friends about Christ.

If You Still Have Time . . .

Friends Indeed—Form groups of no more than five. Have groups each create one skit showing a good way to tell a friend about Christ and one skit showing a poor way. Have groups perform their skits. Then discuss the effectiveness of each way kids present.

Lost Friends?—Form a circle and have kids discuss how comfortable they feel about telling friends about their faith. Have kids discuss how they'd feel if, because of their openness about their faith, friends stopped spending time with them. Have kids brainstorm ways to tell friends about their faith without "turning them off."

RELATIONSHIPS—*Jesus Style*

Read aloud Luke 5:1-11, 27-28 and John 1:35-51 to see how Jesus reached out through relationships. Then take a look at the relationship web below and think about how you relate to friends.

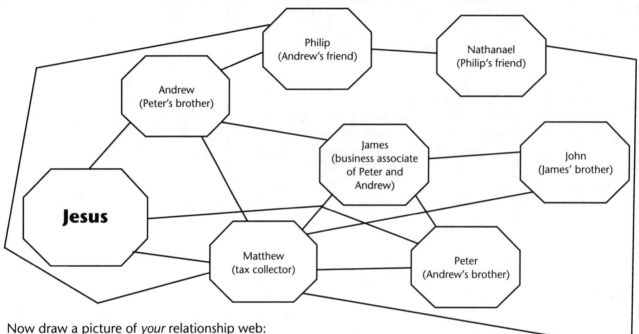

Now draw a picture of *your* relationship web:

● How can you reach out to others through your relationship web?

● How can you involve your friends in your faith?

● Write one thing you'll do this week to let a friend see your faith in action.

Table Talk

To the Parent: We're involved in a junior high course at church called *Telling Your Friends About Christ*. We'd like you and your teenager to spend some time discussing this important topic. Use this "Table Talk" activity to help you do that.

Parent and junior higher
Complete the following sentences:
- I first heard about Jesus when . . .
- I first understood the gospel message when . . .
- When I think of my faith, I feel . . .
- One time I told someone about my faith was . . .
- Someone I know who I could tell about Jesus is . . .

Talk about:
- the most effective way you've seen someone tell others about Christ.
- the most ineffective way you've seen someone tell others about Christ.

Discuss:
- Who needs Jesus Christ?
- How does someone get eternal life?

Do:
Together, think of ways you can tell others about your faith. Then plan specific ways you'll each tell someone about Christ. During the coming week, follow through on your plans.
Afterward, discuss:
- What was positive about the experience?
- What could've been done differently?
- What are new questions you have as a result of this experience?
Then pray for the people you shared your faith with.

Together, read Exodus 15:2; John 3:16; and Acts 4:12. Discuss how the verses make you feel about your faith.

TELLING Your Friends ABOUT CHRIST

LESSON 2

CAUGHT IN A WEB OF LOVE

According to a major study, 55 percent of Christian kids say they want to know how to make a difference in the world. Despite these encouraging statistics, kids don't often know what they can do to make a difference.

By learning that Jesus calls them to take his message to all people, kids can discover a great way to make a difference in the world: taking the good news to non-Christians.

LESSON AIM

To help kids understand how to reach out in love to others.

OBJECTIVES

Students will:
● understand the importance of openly identifying with Christ;
● practice telling how being Christian has made a difference for them;
● identify ways to show love to non-Christian friends; and
● commit to show Christ's love to others.

BIBLE BASIS

MATTHEW 20:26-28
ROMANS 10:13-15
PHILIPPIANS 2:3-4

Look up the following scriptures. Then read the background paragraphs to see how the passages relate to your junior highers and middle schoolers.

In **Matthew 20:26-28** and **Philippians 2:3-4**, we learn that Jesus ministers by meeting needs and preaching.

It's not enough to talk about Jesus. Christians need to let their lives be "walking sermons." Someone once said: "There are two obstacles for non-Christians in coming to Christ. One is that some don't know a Christian and the other is that some do."

Kids need to see that their lives speak louder than their words. As they look at Jesus' life, they'll see how important it is to reach out to their friends in humility, kindness, service and truth. And when their actions match their words, Christian kids will become more effective in telling friends about Christ.

In **Romans 10:13-15**, Paul emphasizes that non-Christians must hear the Word of God before they can respond to it.

It's easy for Christians to think they've "done their duty" to their non-Christian friends just by "living the Christian life." In these verses, Paul asserts being an example isn't enough.

Although it's crucial to demonstrate what it means to be a Christian, people can't respond to God's offer of eternal life if they don't hear about it. Kids need to see that God has "sent" them to their friends and family to deliver his truth.

THIS LESSON AT A GLANCE

Section	Minutes	What Students Will Do	Supplies
Opener (Option 1)	5 to 10	**Undercover Christian**—Learn the importance of identifying with Christ.	3×5 cards, marker, Bible
(Option 2)		**Super Sleuth**—Play a game and learn the importance of telling non-Christians all the facts about Christ.	"Super-Sleuth" clues (p. 27), scissors, envelopes, Bible
Action and Reflection	15 to 20	**Before and After**—Explore how things change when people become Christians.	"Before and After" hand-outs (p. 28), paper, pencils
Bible Application	10 to 15	**Relationship ABCs**—List ways they can show Christ's love to friends.	Bibles, construction paper, markers, tape
Commitment	5 to 10	**Christ-Aid**—Commit to give Christ's love to non-Christians.	Band-Aids, markers, world globe or map, "On Fire" handout (p. 26)
Closing (Option 1)	up to 5	**I Need You**—Describe how they need each other.	Bible, ball of yarn
(Option 2)		**Tell Me What You Think**—Describe ways they see Christ in each other.	

The Lesson

☐ OPTION 1: UNDERCOVER CHRISTIAN

Write the word "Spy" on enough 3×5 cards for everyone but one person to have one. On one card, write, "You're the inventor. When you hear the rules for the game, ignore them. Whatever you say or do, don't reveal yourself to the spies. Act as if you're a spy, too." Distribute a card to each person, and instruct kids not to reveal their cards to each other.

Say: **We're going to play "I Spy." One person here just invented a new source of energy that is more powerful, efficient and cheap than all gas, oil and nuclear energy. These other forms of energy would be completely unnecessary if this new source of energy were introduced to society. The spies must search for the inventor by asking the following two questions: "How does this new energy source work?" and "What is this new energy source?" Only the inventor will know the answer to these questions. You have two minutes, so go!**

After two minutes, stop the game. Ask kids to identify the inventor. After several guesses, have the real inventor come forward.

Ask:

● **Why was it difficult to find the inventor?** (Because no one ever answered the questions; the inventor didn't tell the truth.)

● **How is the way the inventor acted like the way some Christians act?** (Some Christians don't want others to know they're Christians; some Christians act like they aren't Christians.)

● **How are we sometimes undercover Christians with our friends?** (We don't talk about Jesus; we're embarrassed about going to youth group and stuff.)

● **Why are people sometimes afraid to tell others about Christ?** (They're afraid of rejection; they don't want to turn people off; they don't know what to say.)

Read aloud Romans 10:13-15.

Say: **Today we're going to discover ways to overcome our fears so we can tell our friends about Christ.**

☐ OPTION 2: SUPER SLEUTH

Make three photocopies of the "Super-Sleuth" clues handout (p. 27), and cut apart the clues. Insert each set of clues in a different envelope. The clues are incomplete; the mystery can't be solved.

Form three groups. Give each group a Super-Sleuth envelope.

Say: **Felix Farmer was murdered! And your group must determine who the murderer is. You have three minutes to solve the mystery, using the clues in your envelope. When I call time, you'll get only one guess to solve the mystery. And you must give sound proof for your conclusions.**

After three minutes, stop the game. Ask groups to say who they think murdered Felix. After groups have each guessed, say: **None of you are right. Sammy Shotgun killed Felix.**

Ask:

● **Why couldn't you solve the mystery?** (We didn't have all the clues; we didn't know everything we needed to know.)

● **How did you feel when you realized you didn't have all the facts to solve the mystery?** (Frustrated; angry, it was unfair.)

● **How can non-Christians make decisions about Christ if they don't have all the facts about him?** (They can't; nobody can have all the facts.)

Read aloud Romans 10:13-15.

Say: **Just as you didn't have all the clues you needed to solve the mystery, our friends can't solve the mystery of Christianity without hearing about Christ. And God wants us to give our friends enough knowledge to make their own decisions about following Christ.**

Table Talk Follow-Up

If you sent the "Table Talk" handout (p. 19) to parents last week, discuss students' reactions to the activity. Ask volunteers to tell what they learned from the discussion with their parents.

BEFORE AND AFTER

Form two teams—a "Before" team and an "After" team. Say: **We're going to play a game to see which team can find specific items in this room. I'll give each team a clue to help in the search. When a team successfully brings the items to me, that team will be the winner.**

Have the Before team leave the room while you give your clue to the After team. Be sure no one from the Before team can hear what you say. (You may want to write the clue on a sheet of paper and show it to them.) The clue: **I'm looking for four different things that start with the letter "R." Any four will do. The other team won't really know what they're looking for, so play along for a while as you "search" for things around the church. Don't let the other team find out the clue.**

Then have the After team leave the room and invite the Before team in. Give the Before team this clue: **The things I'm looking for come in all shapes and sizes and many different colors. But I only want the right ones.**

ACTION AND REFLECTION
(15 to 20 minutes)

Invite the After team back into the room and start the game. When the After team brings four items beginning with the letter "R" to you, declare that team the winner. Don't tell the other team what made the items correct. Play again, giving similar clues to each group, but using a different letter of the alphabet. Members of the Before team will probably suspect something isn't fair and could become frustrated or angry. That's okay. You'll be discussing kids' feelings after the game. If time permits, play a third round.

There's a slim chance the Before team could guess correctly and bring items that would make it the winning team. If this happens, declare that team the winner of the round and play again. After the rounds are over, discuss how, as in this game, people may accidentally discover God; but that more often, it's because Christians have told them about Christ.

After the game let the Before team in on the correct clues. Then ask the Before team:

● **How did you feel as you played the game?** (Frustrated; angry; it wasn't fair; we didn't have enough information.)

● **How do you feel now, knowing the other team had more information than you?** (Angry; frustrated; it wasn't fair.)

Ask the After team:

● **How did you feel playing the game?** (Confident; frustrated; sad for the other team.)

Ask everyone:

● **If we think of the items you were searching for as a "relationship with God," how is the Before team like a non-Christian?** (The Before team didn't know where to look for God; no one told the Before team about God.)

● **How was the After team like a Christian?** (The After team knew God.)

Say: **If you were on the Before team, you may've felt frustrated or even angry. That's how some non-Christians feel when they're trying to find meaning in life. They don't have enough information to know that meaning is found in a relationship with God.**

Ask:

● **What could the After team have done to help the Before team find the objects?** (Tell them what they knew; show them the objects.)

● **How is that like what Christians can do to help non-Christians discover a relationship with God?** (We can tell them about faith; we can show them our own faith.)

Say: **In case you haven't guessed, the team names re-present Before becoming a Christian and After becoming a Christian. As Christians, we're called to help as many people as possible join the After team.**

Give kids each a "Before and After" handout (p. 28) and a pencil. Have kids each complete the handout. Then form pairs and have partners discuss their handouts.

Form a circle. Ask for volunteers to tell something they learned from the handout or the discussion with their partner.

Say: **When we become Christians, we don't automatically become perfect. Instead, we begin a relationship with God that will develop and grow over time—just like a friendship can grow over time. We can learn from the Bible how our relationships with friends can help them develop a relationship with God, too.**

RELATIONSHIP ABCs

Write the letters of the alphabet each on a separate sheet of construction paper. Shuffle the papers. Form groups of no more than five. Distribute all the alphabet papers evenly among the groups. Give groups each a Bible. Have groups each sit down and read aloud the following scriptures: Matthew 20:26-28; Mark 6:54-56; Luke 8:1; and Philippians 2:3-4.

Tell groups to brainstorm and write on each alphabet paper one thing they can do to build good relationships, based on the scripture passages. For example, kids may write: "**A**ccept my friends even if I disagree with them"; "**B**e there for my friends"; "**C**are about others' problems." Tell kids they can substitute "ex" for the letter "X."

When groups are finished, call out each letter of the alphabet in order. Have the group with that letter stand and read together the relationship-builder, then tape the letter to the wall. When all the letters are on the wall, have kids form a semi-circle facing the letters.

Ask:

● **How can the way we relate to our friends help them know Christ's love?** (We can be examples of Christ's love; we can tell our friends about Christ; we can model good behavior.)

Say: **Today we've seen how non-Christians will never know about God's love unless someone tells them. Well, guess what . . . we're that someone.**

CHRIST-AID

Give kids each a Band Aid and a marker. Have them each write "Christ" on their Band Aid. Place a globe or map of the world at the front of the room.

Say: **Mother Teresa said, "The hunger for love is much more difficult to remove than the hunger for bread." There's a famine in the land, and only Christ can fill that hunger.**

Many of you have heard of Live-Aid for world hunger and Farm-Aid for farmers' financial needs. Today we're going to have Christ-Aid.

Have kids each place their "Christ-Aid" on the globe as they complete this sentence: "I will give Christ to a lost and hurting world by . . ." Be sure the Band-Aids don't ruin the globe or map.

**B I B L E
A P P L I C A T I O N**
(10 to 15 minutes)

C O M M I T M E N T
(5 to 10 minutes)

Give kids each a copy of the "On Fire" handout in the margin below. Have kids each read it and carry it with them in their wallet or purse to help them know how to talk with friends about faith.

CLOSING
(up to 5 minutes)

☐ OPTION 1: I NEED YOU
Form a circle, and read aloud John 13:35.

Say: **We need each other to show Christ's love to our world.**

Holding the loose end of a ball of yarn, throw the rest of the ball to someone in the group and complete this sentence: **"(Name), I need your (describe a positive trait such as faith, kindness or warmth) to show Christ's love to the world."** Have kids continue around the circle until everyone is part of Christ's web of love." Close with prayer, asking God to fill your group with love for one another and others outside of the group.

On Fire

Use this card for ideas on how to start a conversation about faith.

● **Family**—What kind of church involvement has your family had? What do your family members believe about God?

● **Interests**—What kinds of things do you like to do on Sundays? Have you ever been interested in reading the Bible? Why or why not?

● **Religion**—What do you think about religion? What do you think God is like?

● **Experiences**—What do you think about religious experiences? How do you think God talks to people? How do you feel about prayer?

☐ OPTION 2: TELL ME WHAT YOU THINK
Form a circle. Have kids each pick a letter from the Relationship ABCs that describes the person on their right. Have the person who's wearing the brightest-color clothes turn to the person on his or her right and complete this sentence: "You have _____ me. Share your _____ with others." For example, someone might say, "You have encouraged me. Share your encouragement with others." Move clockwise around the circle until kids each have said something positive about the person on their right.

Close with prayer, asking God to support each person's efforts to tell friends about Christ's love.

If You Still Have Time . . .
Objection Overruled—One at a time, read the following objections people give about Christianity. Then have kids read the related scripture verses and discuss how they'd respond to people with each objection.

● **What about the hypocrites in the church?** Romans 2:1, 14:12
● **I'd have to give up too much to be a Christian.** Mark 8:36 and Philippians 3:7-8
● **Why does a loving God allow so much evil in the world?** Romans 8:18 and 1 John 5:19
● **I'm good enough without becoming a Christian.** John 3:3 and Ephesians 2:8-9
● **The Bible is just a bunch of myths.** John 12:48 and 2 Peter 1:20-21

Telling Poems—Form groups of no more than five. Assign each group one of the following topics: what a Christian might say to a non-Christian about faith; what a non-Christian might say about a Christian's explanation of faith; what Jesus might say to a non-Christian today. Have groups each brainstorm ideas for their topic and write a short poem to describe one or more of their ideas. For example, a group might write a poem about a non-Christian who mocks a Christian's faith. Have groups each read their poem. Then discuss the poems.

SUPER-SLEUTH

Photocopy and cut apart these clues. Put each set of clues in a separate envelope.

Mystery: Felix Farmer was found fallen in the fodder while feeding a new foal. Who flailed Felix?

Clue: Barney Barnstormer wasn't fond of Frieda Farmer.

Clue: Barney Barnstormer often loaned his pitchfork to Felix Farmer.

Clue: The pitchfork was flung beside fallen Felix.

Clue: Barney Barnstormer often visited Trevor Tractor on Saturdays.

Clue: Frieda Farmer had just found the lost cow when Officer Orville found the felled Felix.

Clue: Beatrice Barnstormer only made bacon on weekends.

Clue: Beatrice Barnstormer didn't know the cow was missing.

Clue: Trevor Tractor was out of town when Felix was flailed.

Clue: Barney Barnstormer owned the only pitchfork in the county.

Clue: Frieda Farmer was angry at Felix for letting the cow out on a Saturday.

Clue: When Felix was found by Officer Orville, the smell of bacon was wafting from Beatrice Barnstormer's kitchen.

Clue: The bacon was burned.

Clue: Barney Barnstormer liked his bacon undercooked.

Clue: Barney Barnstormer was dressed in his Sunday best when Frieda Farmer found the cow.

BEFORE AND AFTER

What changes when you become a Christian? Write your answers to the questions below then find a partner and discuss your answers.

   When you become a Christian, what (if anything) is different about your:

- attitude?

- behavior?

- habits?

- relationships with friends?

- relationships with family members?

   Does becoming a Christian mean you won't sin anymore? Explain.

   In 10 words or less, describe what it's like to become a Christian.

   Write how you feel when you hear people describe Christians as:

- holy rollers.

- weak people.

- hypocrites.

   What's the best thing that happens when you become a Christian?

BRIDGE-BUILDING

Grant's palms grew clammy; his throat was parched; his heart beat rapidly; and his lips quivered. His "fight or flight" instinct was kicking in, and all he wanted to do was fly!

What horrible threat was Grant facing? His friend Mike had just asked him, "What does it mean to be a Christian, anyway?"

Although kids want to tell others about Christ, they sometimes just don't know what to say. Kids need to be equipped with the tools to share their faith.

To help kids know how to tell others about God's love.

Students will:
- **identify questions non-Christians may have about Christ;**
- **realize the importance of knowing what they believe; and**
- **learn how to tell others about Christ.**

Look up the following scriptures. Then read the background paragraphs to see how the passages relate to your junior highers and middle schoolers.

In **John 3:16**, Jesus explains God's motive for sending Jesus to Earth: love.

Rather than seeing Christianity as an exclusive club, kids need to see it as an inclusive family where God the father loves his children. God didn't send Jesus to condemn the world, but to save it. Kids need to get a glimpse of how God's heart breaks for the children who haven't yet come into his family.

In **1 Corinthians 15:3-4**, Paul explains the essence of Jesus' message.

Nowhere else in scripture is Jesus' message so succinctly presented. Paul didn't want his readers to miss what he was

LESSON AIM

OBJECTIVES

BIBLE BASIS
JOHN 3:16
1 CORINTHIANS 15:3-4

telling them. In so doing, Paul described what is essential for Christians to believe.

Paul explained that Christ died for our sins, that he was buried and that he was raised again on the third day, fulfilling scriptural prophecy. Based on believing these essentials, people either follow Christ in faith or choose to reject him. Kids need to understand these essentials as they tell their friends about Christ.

THIS LESSON AT A GLANCE

Section	Minutes	What Students Will Do	Supplies
Opener (Option 1)	5 to 10	**What's a Frabbistat?**—Brainstorm questions people might ask about a made-up object.	Paper, pencils, Bibles
(Option 2)		**Try Christianity**—Make posters advertising Christianity.	Posterboard, markers, magazines, tape
Action and Reflection	10 to 15	**Why?**—Explain what they believe and why.	
Bible Application	10 to 15	**Faith Essentials**—Practice telling others about Christ.	Bibles, newsprint, marker, "What U Need 2 Know" handouts (p. 35), pencils, paper
Commitment	5 to 10	**Broken Bread**—Encourage each other to tell friends about Christ.	3×5 cards, tape, pencils, bread
Closing (Option 1)	5 to 10	**Awards Ceremony**—Receive awards for strengths in telling others about Christ.	Small toys or gifts
(Option 2)		**Commissioning Service**—Pray for each other to be effective in telling others about Christ.	

The Lesson

OPENER
(5 to 10 minutes)

☐ OPTION 1: WHAT'S A FRABBISTAT?

Form groups of no more than four. Give groups each paper and pencils.

Say: **I have just invented the amazing, incredible, never-before-seen-on-TV frabbistat! And you're going to help me sell it. In your groups, lists some questions potential buyers might ask about the frabbistat.**

Don't tell kids anything more about the frabbistat. After a few minutes, have groups each show their list to the whole class.

Ask:

● **How easy was it to make your list? Explain.** (It was easy, you just need to ask lots of different kinds of questions; it was very difficult, I didn't know where to begin.)

● **How are these questions similar to or different from the questions a non-Christian might have about Christ?** (They're similar, non-Christians don't know what kinds of questions to ask; they're different, non-Christians know exactly what they want to know.)

● **How is explaining your belief in Christ like or unlike selling something?** (Similar, you have to convince people of the value of both; different, talking about our beliefs shouldn't be like selling used cars.)

Give groups each another sheet of paper and have them work together to quickly draw a frabbistat. Don't tell kids what a frabbistat looks like. (In case you're wondering: There's no such thing.) After a couple of minutes, have groups each present their illustration. Kids will probably have very different pictures of what a frabbistat looks like.

Ask:

● **How easy was it to draw the frabbistat? Explain.** (Easy, I made it whatever I wanted it to look like; impossible, we don't know what one looks like.)

Say: **It would be nearly impossible for us to sell a frabbistat to someone who asked all the questions you brainstormed, since none of us knows what one is. In the same way, if we don't understand what it means to be Christian, we can't very easily tell others about Christ.**

Say: **Today we're going to take a look at what we need to know before we tell our friends about Christ.**

☐ OPTION 2: TRY CHRISTIANITY

Form groups of no more than three. Distribute posterboard and markers to each group. Have groups each design a poster advertising Christianity. Tell them to consider themes such as: Jesus came to save the world; Christians have more fun; Jesus forgives sins. Have groups look through magazines for ideas on how to create an advertisement. Encourage them to copy advertising styles they like.

When they're done, have groups each tape their poster to the wall.

Ask:

● **Based on these posters alone, would non-Christians want to become Christians? Why or why not?** (Yes, they'd see what Jesus does for them; no, they wouldn't be interested.)

● **Was it easy to create a poster advertising Christianity? Why or why not?** (Yes, I knew just what to say to a non-

Christian; no, faith isn't easy to put on paper.)

● **How is creating this poster like trying to tell someone about your faith?** (It's difficult to do; you need to know what you'll say.)

Say: **Today we're going to explore what you need to know before you tell someone about your faith.**

WHY?

Form groups of no more than three. Have kids each take a turn explaining their beliefs to the other members of their group. Have the first volunteer in each group make a statement of his or her beliefs; for example, "I believe in God." Then have the other group members ask "Why?" after each statement the person makes. Tell kids they must try to answer the "why" questions and that "because" isn't a good enough answer. Allow this to continue for three minutes. Then have another person take the volunteer's place and continue the process.

Afterward, ask:

● **When people kept asking "Why?" how did you feel?** (Nervous; uncomfortable; angry.)

● **How is this like the way you feel when trying to explain your beliefs to your friends?** (It's the same, I get real nervous; it's different, my friends don't badger me; I don't know, I've never talked to them about it.)

● **What things did you find difficult to explain about your beliefs?** (I don't know much about my faith; all I remember about my faith is what someone else has told me; I feel uncomfortable talking about my faith.)

Say: **Sometimes it's hard to explain our belief in Christ to non-Christians. We're going to learn an easy way to tell our friends about Christ.**

FAITH ESSENTIALS

Form pairs, and give them each paper and pencils. Ask partners to determine together the essentials of Christianity. Have them use the paper and pencils to keep track of their ideas. After a few minutes, have a volunteer read aloud John 3:16 and 1 Corinthians 15:3-4. List the following items on newsprint while the volunteer reads the verses: God's love, Jesus, faith, eternal life, death, Resurrection.

Ask:

● **Are there other essentials of Christianity that aren't listed here?**

Write kids' answers on the newsprint.

Say: **For a mechanic to effectively work on a car or a surgeon to effectively perform open-heart surgery, he or she needs the best tools. One way you can be effective in telling your friends about Christ is by using the "What U Need 2 Know" presentation.**

Using the "What U Need 2 Know" handout (p. 35), copy each step onto newsprint as you explain it. Read each step aloud and answer questions kids have about it. Then distribute the handouts, pencils and paper. Have partners practice using the presentation with each other.

After partners each have practiced the presentation, ask:

● **What do you think of this presentation?** (It's okay; it's silly; it's too canned.)

● **How do you feel about having a tool like this to use for telling your friends about Christ?** (Good, it'll help when I don't know what to say; I don't like it, it'll sound too rehearsed.)

Read aloud John 16:8-14. Say: **You're not alone when you tell friends about Christ. The Holy Spirit prepares people's hearts to hear the truth. You don't have to use the exact words in the "What U Need 2 Know" presentation. Just remember the essentials of Christianity when you're talking with your friends about faith in Christ, and trust the Holy Spirit to help.**

BROKEN BREAD

Give each person a 3×5 card and a pencil. Have them each write on their card the name of a person they want to tell about Christ. Give kids each a piece of tape, and have them tape their card to their chest.

Form a circle. Break a piece off a loaf of bread and turn to the person on your right. Give the remaining loaf to the person as you say: **This is Christ's body broken for you to share with** (say the name on the person's card).

Continue until the bread goes all the way around the circle. Then have kids each tell one thing they'll do in the coming weeks to tell friends about Christ. For example, someone might say: "I'm going to invite a friend to church next week" or "I'm going to talk with a friend about what he or she believes." Encourage kids to call one another on the phone during the week and talk about how things are going as they learn to tell friends about Christ.

☐ OPTION 1: AWARDS CEREMONY

Get small toys or small gifts to give as awards for each of your class members. Try to think of specific positive things you've seen in each student and pick an appropriate gift that relates to his or her ability or willingness to tell others about Christ. Some examples of awards: a salt-shaker for creating a "thirst" for Jesus, a fishing lure for actively "reeling" people in to Jesus, or a mirror for "reflecting" God's love to people. Be creative.

Create an awards-ceremony atmosphere by having kids sit in chairs while you stand at the front of the room. As you give each award, have that person come to the front of the room to

COMMITMENT
(5 to 10 minutes)

CLOSING
(5 to 10 minutes)

receive it. Have kids applaud after each award is given.

After everyone receives an award, form a circle and have kids place their arms around each other for a group hug.

☐ OPTION 2: COMMISSIONING SERVICE

Form a circle and put a chair in the middle of the circle. Have kids take turns sitting in the chair. As each person sits in the chair, say: **God has given you a great command: to tell others about Christ. And he's given you the ability to follow his command.** Then have groups members call out abilities the person in the center of the circle has that'll help him or her tell friends about Christ; for example: patience, friendliness, caring attitude, strong faith.

After each person has been in the center of the circle, have volunteers close in prayer, asking God for the desire to know more about faith and the ability to tell friends about Christ.

If You Still Have Time . . .

Charades—Write one of the following words each on a separate 3×5 card: friend, neighbor, teacher, stranger, school-bus driver, parent, sister, brother. Give kids each a card. Have kids each perform a charade to help others guess who the person on their card is. Then discuss specific ways to tell that person about Christ.

Salty T-Shirts—Have kids work together to choose a youth group name and logo that identifies the group as Christian. For example, kids might suggest "God Squad" or "Salt of the Earth." Have kids draw the name and logo big enough to fill the front of a T-shirt. Then work with kids to get the design printed on T-shirts. Or provide fabric paints and plain T-shirts so kids can make their own T-shirts. Discuss how something as simple as a T-shirt might prompt a discussion with a non-Christian about faith.

WHAT U NEED 2 KNOW

Consider this approach when telling a friend about Christ. Remember, your style of telling others about Christ will be different from someone else's. Don't try to be someone you aren't. Just be yourself and tell your friend these four basic points. Read the scripture verses to better understand where each basic point comes from. And always remember to pray for God's help as you tell others about Christ.

L ove — The Bible says God loves us and wants us to experience full life (John 10:10).

O wn way — But instead of following God, the Bible says we began to sin and to go our own way. We wanted to be our own bosses (Isaiah 53:6).

R esult — Sin resulted in separation from God. So instead of having a full life on Earth and eternal life in heaven, the Bible says we were dead spiritually and would've always been separated from God (Ephesians 2:1-5).

D elight — But because of God's love for us, he sent Jesus Christ to die on a cross to pay the penalty for our sins. On the third day, Jesus was raised from the dead and bridged the gap to God. All who believe in Jesus will become children of God and have the full and eternal life God wants for all people (John 1:12).

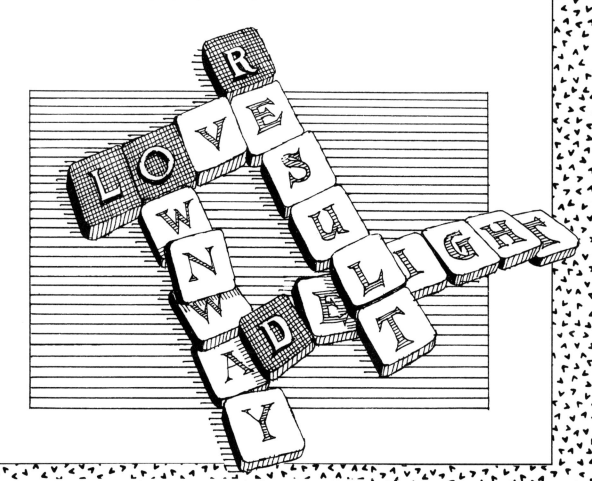

LESSON 4

LOOK WHO'S TALKING

Kids don't know how to tell others about their Christian faith. Some kids feel comfortable "preaching" to their friends while others are scared to say anything at all. By learning how Jesus reached out to people through relationships, kids can discover new ways to tell others about Christ through their own relationships.

LESSON AIM

To help kids each develop their own style of telling others about Christ.

OBJECTIVES

Students will:
● understand they can make a difference in their world;
● evaluate different styles of telling others about Christ;
● choose which style they are most comfortable with; and
● commit to let their light shine.

BIBLE BASIS
MATTHEW 16:13-19
JOHN 3:1—4:54

Look up the following scriptures. Then read the background paragraphs to see how the passages relate to your junior highers and middle schoolers.

In **Matthew 16:13-19,** Jesus says that God is the only one who can reveal truth to people.

During his Earthly ministry, people had different opinions of who Jesus was. Some said he was John the Baptist, Elijah or Jeremiah raised from the dead. People saw the miracles in Jesus' ministry and tried to explain them away. But it was Peter who saw the truth clearly and declared, "You are the Christ, the son of the living God." Then Jesus promised to build the church person by person.

Christian kids can learn to see themselves as construction tools and to see God as the builder. As tools in God's hands, kids can be confident in telling others about their faith. They can reflect Christ and his truth—and God will take care of the rest.

In **John 3:1—4:54**, Jesus leads several different people to faith in himself.

Jesus helped many people understand his mission. The disciples, Nicodemus, the woman at the well, the royal official and others encountered Jesus and became believers. Jesus met each person's deepest needs and answered searching questions. Whether on a mountainside, in a boat or in the middle of a swarming city, Jesus reached out to people.

Teenagers have seen people use different styles of telling others about Christ and aren't always sure which style is best for them. By seeing how Jesus related to people, kids can each develop their own style based on how they relate to others.

THIS LESSON AT A GLANCE

Section	Minutes	What Students Will Do	Supplies
Opener (Option 1)	5 to 10	**Salt of the Earth**—Create pictures and direct their partners to blindly reproduce them.	Salt, cups, construction paper, Bible
(Option 2)		**Light of the World**—Discuss how they're the light of the world.	Flashlight, basket, Bible
Action and Reflection	10 to 15	**In This Corner**—Evaluate different styles of telling others about Christ.	Construction paper, tape
Bible Application	10 to 15	**Campaign for Jesus**—Decide which style of telling others about Christ is most like theirs.	"Campaign for Jesus" handouts (p. 43), Bibles, "Telling Others" handouts (p. 44), pencils
Commitment	5 to 10	**Candle Circle**—Commit to tell a non-Christian friend about Christ.	Large candle, small candles, matches, cardboard
Closing (Option 1)	5 to 10	**Name-Calling**—Write on cards qualities they see in each other.	3×5 cards, markers, tape
(Option 2)		**Upon This Rock**—Identify friends who need Christ and build a monument to Christ.	Bible, rocks, markers

The Lesson

OPENER

(5 to 10 minutes)

☐ OPTION 1: SALT OF THE EARTH

Give kids each a sheet of construction paper and a cup half-filled with salt. Form pairs, and have partners sit back to back. Have the partner in each pair whose birthday is closest to yours use salt to "draw" a picture on the construction paper. Be sure the other partners don't look at the "drawings." Tell kids they can draw any picture they want. When the first partners finish their salt pictures, say: **Now, the first partners each must describe their drawing so the second partner can use his or her sand and copy it. Partners may not look at each other's drawings—only verbal instructions are allowed.**

When partners finish, ask:

● **How easy was it to reproduce your partner's picture?** (Not very easy, I kept wanting to turn around and look; easy, my partner gave great directions.)

● **Would your pictures have matched better if you could've seen the original? Why or why not?** (Yes, words just aren't enough sometimes; yes, I could've understood better if I could've seen the real thing.)

● **How is this exercise like or unlike telling people about Christ?** (It's like it, because people need to see our lives and not just hear our words; it's unlike it, because people always see our lives when we're talking to them.)

Read aloud Matthew 5:13-16.

Say: **You are the salt of the Earth. Today we're going to talk about how you can add flavor to your relationships by telling others about Christ's love.**

☐ OPTION 2: LIGHT OF THE WORLD

Have the lights out when kids arrive. If the room you usually meet in isn't easily darkened, plan to meet in a dark room for this opening activity. Place a turned-on flashlight under an overturned wicker basket in the center of the room. Have kids form a circle around the basket. Read aloud Matthew 5:14-16.

Ask kids to describe what they can see in the dim light. Give them a couple of minutes to describe their surroundings as accurately as possible.

Then have a volunteer take the flashlight from under the basket and shine it around the room. Have kids describe what more they can see with the flashlight shining around the room. Then turn on the lights.

Ask:

● **How was it easier to see the things in the room when**

the flashlight was taken out from under the basket? (We could point at specific things and see them better; the light wasn't hidden.)

● **Why does Jesus compare us to light?** (We reveal things; we shine in the darkness; we lead the way.)

● **How do Christians hide their light?** (By not doing good things; by not revealing Christ.)

● **How is shining the flashlight around the room like letting the light of your Christian faith shine for others?** (The flashlight makes things easier to see, just as telling others about Christ helps them see God's love; the light brightens the room just as we can brighten others' lives.)

Say: **Our lives are the light of Christ in a dark world. Today we're going to talk about how we can let our lives shine.**

IN THIS CORNER

Tape a red construction paper circle in one corner of the room, a green circle in another corner and a yellow circle in another corner. Have kids stand in the center of the room.

Say: **I'm going to read a list of ways people tell others about Christ. After I read each item, go to one of the three corners, depending on whether you think it's an effective way to tell others about Christ. Red means "stop—it'll never work," yellow means "caution—it might work" and green means "go for it."**

After each item, have kids discuss in their corners why they selected that color. Then call on specific kids to tell what was discussed in their groups. Choose different kids each time.

Read the following ways:
● **Wearing a T-shirt that says "Jesus Saves";**
● **Helping a new guy find his classes at school;**
● **Going to church;**
● **Carrying a Bible in your jeans pocket;**
● **Using a megaphone to preach in front of your school;**
● **Cheating on an exam;**
● **Telling something you've learned from the Bible to a friend during lunch period;**
● **Describing a way Jesus makes a difference in your life to a teacher during class;**
● **Leaving a flier about Jesus instead of money as a waitress' tip;**
● **Not following through on commitments;**
● **Inviting someone to a youth group party;**
● **Not drinking at a party; and**
● **Going from house to house to tell people about Christ.**

Have kids return to their seats and ask:
● **How did you feel as you chose which corner to stand in? Explain.** (Confused, I didn't know how to respond;

ACTION AND REFLECTION
(10 to 15 minutes)

anxious, I didn't want to look stupid and choose the wrong corner; confident, I knew which answer I thought was right.)

● **How did you feel when I called on you to tell what you'd discussed?** (Embarrassed; uncomfortable; confident.)

● **How are these feelings like the feelings people have when they wonder how to tell others about Christ?** (Some people feel confident telling others about Christ; some people feel uncomfortable.)

Say: **People disagree on what's the most effective way to tell someone about Christ. What works for you may not work for someone else. Next we'll look at the styles some people from the Bible used, and choose which style is most like our own.**

BIBLE APPLICATION
(10 to 15 minutes)

CAMPAIGN FOR JESUS

Form five groups. A group can be one person. Give each group a Bible and a different "Campaign for Jesus" button from the handout (p. 43). Have groups each study their button and read the scripture passage listed.

Say: **We're having an election for the savior of the world. We all know the savior of the world is Jesus, but there are many people who don't know that. Your group will have up to two minutes to present reasons people should become Christians. Use the ideas and suggestions on your group's campaign button to create your presentation. We'll vote afterward on the presentation we liked best.**

Give groups five minutes to read their scriptures and talk about their presentations. Then have groups each present their campaign speech. For example, the "woman at the well" group might talk about the experience of meeting Jesus and how his compassion makes him a perfect candidate for being our savior.

Afterward, ask:

● **Which group was most effective in campaigning for Jesus? Explain.** (The John group, the kids were gentle and convinced me about Jesus' love; the Thomas group; the kids gave good reasons to believe in Jesus.)

● **Which group was least effective in campaigning for Jesus? Explain.** (The Peter group, the kids were too aggressive; the Joseph group, the kids never even mentioned Jesus' name.)

● **Which group best characterizes your "campaigning" style?**

Form pairs. Give partners each a "Telling Others" handout (p. 44) and a pencil. Have kids each complete the handout and discuss it with their partner.

Form a circle and have kids each tell something good they learned about their partner during the discussion time. For example, kids might say, "My partner does a good job of telling others about Christ" or "My partner is really excited to tell others about Christ." Remind kids to be positive.

Say: **You don't need to feel bad if you're not like Peter. Some of us are more like Joseph or the woman at the well. Using methods of telling others about Christ that fit each of us best is the best way to go about it. Just as people in Jesus' time had different ways to tell others about Jesus, we each have a different approach to telling friends about Christ.**

CANDLE CIRCLE

Form a circle, and place a large candle on the floor in the middle of the circle. Give each person a small candle with a cardboard circle around it to catch dripping wax. Turn off the lights, and light the big candle.

Say: **You are the light of the world, but each of you must commit to let your light shine. Think of one non-Christian friend in your life who hasn't seen Christ's light. When it's your turn, light your candle and say a silent prayer for your non-Christian friend.**

To start, step forward and light your candle. Continue around the circle until every candle is lit.

When all candles are lit, quietly sing together "They Will Know We Are Christians by Our Love" or another familiar song. Allow a moment of silent prayer following the song.

☐ OPTION 1: NAME-CALLING

Give kids each a 3×5 card and a marker. Have kids each write their name on their 3×5 card. Then form a circle and have kids pass the cards to their left. Tell kids to each write one positive quality on each card as it's passed around the circle; for example: helpful, kind, loving or friendly. Encourage kids to list qualities people have that help them be effective at telling others about Christ.

Then have kids each tape their own card onto their shirt. Have them go around the room and read each other's cards. Close by praying for strength to use the qualities we have to tell others about Christ.

☐ OPTION 2: UPON THIS ROCK

Read aloud Matthew 16:18.

Give kids each a marker and some rocks (each an inch or two across). Be sure to include yourself. Have kids each write on separate rocks the names of people they want to tell about Christ.

Form a circle, and have kids each pass their rocks to the person on their left.

One at a time, have kids place the rocks they've been given on the floor in the center of the circle forming a monument to Christ, such as an altar or a cross. As they each place the

COMMITMENT
(5 to 10 minutes)

CLOSING
(5 to 10 minutes)

rocks on the monument, have them complete this sentence using the name of the person to their right. "(Name), you are a rock, and through you Christ will reach these people."

If You Still Have Time . . .

Patchwork Quilt—Give kids each a sheet of paper and a marker. Have them each draw a symbol representing who they are. Discuss how kids can depend on one another in telling their friends about Christ. Afterward, have kids tape the sheets together to form a patchwork "quilt." Display the quilt in your meeting room for a month as a reminder to work together in telling others about Christ.

Course Reflection—Form a circle. Ask students to reflect on the past four lessons. Have them take turns completing the following sentences:

- Something I learned in this course is . . .
- If I could tell my friends about this course, I'd say . . .
- Something I'll do differently because of this course is . . .

CAMPAIGN FOR JESUS

PETER
ACTS 3:11-26
Read your passage and imagine you're just like Peter.
Be bold and aggressive in your campaign speech.
Speak with a loud voice.
Talk about God's wrath and judgment.
Stress that Jesus calls for repentance from sin.

JOSEPH
JOHN 19:38-42
Discuss how you followed Jesus from afar in your campaign speech.
Tell things you heard him say, such as in his Sermon on the Mount (Matthew 5).
But never mention Jesus' name, because you're a "secret disciple."

JOHN
I JOHN 4:7-11
Discuss Jesus' love for the world in your campaign speech.
Talk about how the world would be different because of Jesus' love.
Tell how you were called "the beloved disciple" because of how Jesus loved you.

Woman at the Well
JOHN 4:7-26
Discuss the experience you had with Jesus in your campaign speech.
Tell how he knew everything about you.
Talk about how he wasn't prejudiced against you.
Stress how he changed your life.

THOMAS
JOHN 20:24-29
Read your passage and imagine you're just like Thomas.
Be logical and academic in your campaign speech.
Talk about how Jesus fulfilled Old Testament prophecies concerning him.
Explain how you once doubted, but Jesus gave you undeniable proof.

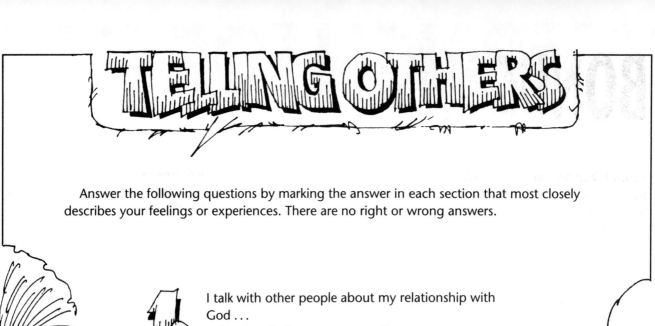

TELLING OTHERS

Answer the following questions by marking the answer in each section that most closely describes your feelings or experiences. There are no right or wrong answers.

 I talk with other people about my relationship with God . . .
- ☐ often (at least once a week).
- ☐ sometimes (every few months).
- ☐ never.

 When I talk about my relationship with God, I feel . . .
- ☐ awkward and unnatural.
- ☐ unprepared.
- ☐ enthused and excited.

 I find it most difficult to talk about my faith in God . . .
- ☐ with kids my own age.
- ☐ with my parents or family.
- ☐ with strangers.

 I find it easiest to talk about my faith in God . . .
- ☐ with kids my own age.
- ☐ with my parents or family.
- ☐ with strangers.

 When I think about Christ's command to "go and make disciples of all nations," I generally feel . . .
- ☐ motivated and excited.
- ☐ guilty and resentful.
- ☐ unprepared, fearful and uneasy.

BONUS IDEAS

Friendship Event—Ask each class member to bring a good friend who isn't a Christian to an event. Have a devotional on friendship. Talk about how Jesus makes a difference in friendships. Play friendship songs such as "Friends" by Michael W. Smith or "Best of Friends" by Billy Crockett.

Have "friendly" refreshments. For example, form pairs and have banana-split races. Tie the hands of one partner in each pair, and have the other partner feed him or her a banana split. Race to see which pair finishes first. Then switch and race again.

Decisions About Friendships—Help junior highers learn ways to relate to non-Christian friends. Plan a meeting or series that walks teenagers through friendship decisions.

As a guide, use the book *A Time to Belong* by Vicki Grove (Teenage Books). When you order six or more copies you receive a free leaders guide. The leaders guide has four complete lessons filled with creative activities, discussion questions and Bible studies.

Survey Says—Have kids develop a survey similar to the one below. Have them ask friends, family members and teachers the questions. Then have kids compile and discuss the results.

Survey Questions:
1. Who is Jesus Christ?
2. Do you believe Jesus rose from the dead? Why or why not?
3. Do you believe Jesus is the only way to God? Why or why not?
4. What makes someone a Christian?
5. If you could ask God any question, what would it be?

Eyewitness News—Have kids videotape creative news stories about Christian faith. After the video is complete, arrange to show it during another class or at a party where there are non-Christian friends. Use the suggestions below to spark more ideas:

● **Interview**—Have someone dress up as an actual witness of Jesus' life during his Earthly ministry. Ask this person questions about what Jesus did, who he said he was, and what resulted from his life, death and Resurrection.

● **News brief**—Summarize one of Jesus' typical days, using scripture. For example, from John 4 the anchor-person could read: "Jesus of Nazareth continued stirring up a commotion

MEETINGS AND MORE

in Samaria. He crossed gender and racial lines today to speak with a Samaritan woman about 'living water.' Afterward, the whole town came running out to see where this living water was coming from.

"From there, he journeyed to Galilee where he was met by a royal official. Witnesses say the man asked Jesus to heal his sick son. The official's son is said to have been healed at the very moment Jesus spoke. Area doctors are still investigating the incident and are declining comment."

● **Sports**—Have a sports broadcaster report on the Lions vs. Christians contest. Have the broadcaster play up the persecution and tremendous faith of the Christians during this time.

● **Special report**—Interrupt a program in progress with a special report. Any story in the gospels would work here. Kids could pretend to be on the scene when Jesus feeds the 5,000 or when Jesus raises Lazarus from the dead.

Eternal Lifesaving Handbook—After the course, have kids compile a handbook of everything they've learned about telling others about Christ. Then have the kids present it to a younger class. Have kids design a lifesaving patch to present to the students in the younger class upon their completion of the Eternal Lifesaving Handbook.

Study Group—Form a study group for kids interested in learning more about telling others about Christ. Use a book for discussion, such as *Screwtape Letters* by C.S. Lewis (Macmillan), *Know What You Believe* by Paul Little (Victor), or *Out of the Saltshaker* by Rebecca Pippert (Inter-Varsity).

Big Event—Have kids plan a large-group activity to expose their non-Christian friends to Christian faith. Rent a film and serve pizza on the lawn; arrange for a local Christian musician to perform; or have a Wacky Olympics. Be sure to include lots of fun crowdbreakers and opportunities for discussing faith issues. Debrief your kids after the activity and focus on the positive things that happened. The results may not be impressive, so help kids see what they learned through the experience and how they helped plant seeds.

Table Talk—Use the "Table Talk" handout (p. 19) as the basis for a meeting. Consider using this as a fifth-week option for the course. Have kids and parents work through the handout together as part of the meeting. Invite parents to describe times they told someone about their faith and the responses they received. Have fun activities for parents and kids to do together. Check out the book *Boredom Busters* by Cindy Hansen (Group Books) for fun game ideas.

Happy Birthday!—Whenever a non-Christian makes a faith commitment, have a wild "New Life" celebration. Bake a birthday cake for the new Christian and write "Happy Birthday in Jesus!" on the cake. Give the person an adoption-into-the-family-of-God certificate. Have kids each bring a baby-shower gag gift with a meaningful bit of advice attached to it. For example, someone could bring a baby bottle and attach a note that says, "Thirst for the pure milk of the Word." Or someone could bring Band-Aids and write "When you fall, Jesus will pick you up and bandage your wounds."

Andrew Dinner—Have kids put on a dinner in honor of Jesus. Have kids each invite a non-Christian friend to the dinner and explain it's in honor of Jesus. During the dinner, have someone share his or her faith story. Play contemporary-Christian music during the meal. Afterward, play games. For fun game ideas, use *Quick Crowdbreakers and Games for Youth Groups* (Group Books).

Faith Gardening—Arrange with a farmer who has a small farm to use the farm for this retreat. Have the farmer talk to kids about what it means to harvest a crop. Have the kids observe the farmer's daily routine and pitch in wherever they can. During the retreat, give kids lots of hands-on experience with the gardening aspect of farming. Use Luke 8:1-15 and the "Nature of Faith-Sharing" handout (p. 48) as a basis for teaching times.

PARTY PLEASERS

RETREAT IDEA

NATURE OF FAITH-SHARING

Complete the following chart to see how you can better cultivate your relationships with non-Christian friends. Use the first item as an example of how to complete the handout.

In Nature	In Scripture	In Life
Early Rains	Colossians 4:5	*Make the most of your opportunities to tell friends about Christ.*
Plowing	Mark 10:45	
Planting	Isaiah 28:23-26	
Late Rains	Isaiah 55:10-11	
Care and Protection	Luke 13:6-9	
Harvest	Matthew 13:23	

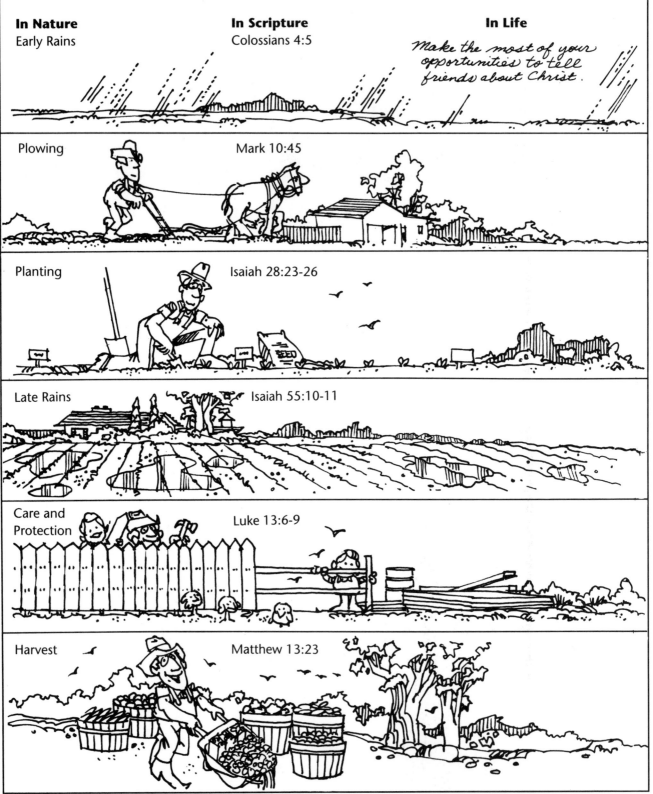